A Guide for Using

From the Mixed-up Files of Mrs. Basil E. Frankweiler

in the Classroom

Based on the novel written by E. L. Konigsburg

This guide written by Mari Lu Robbins
Illustrated by Cheryl Buhler and Penelope Mendivel
Cover Art By Nancee McClure

Teacher Created Materials, In
6421 Industry Way
Westminster, CA 92683
www.teachercreated.com
©1994 Teacher Created Materials, Inc.
Reprinted, 2002
Made in U.S.A.
ISBN 1-55734-448-5

D1465669

Table of Contents

Introduction

Good books are wonderful! They stimulate our imagination, inform our minds, inspire our higher selves, and fill our time with magic! With good books, we are never lonely or bored. And a good book only gets better with time, because each reading brings us new meaning. Each new story is a treasure to cherish forever.

In *Literature Units,* we take great care to select books that will become treasured friends for life.

Teachers using this unit will find the following features to supplement their own valuable ideas.

- Sample Lesson Plans

- Pre-reading Activities

- A Biographical Sketch and Picture of the Author

- A Book Summary

- Vocabulary Lists and Suggested Vocabulary Activities

- Chapters grouped for study, with each section including:

    - *quizzes*

    - *hands-on projects*

    - *cooperative learning activities*

    - *cross-curriculum connections*

    - *extensions into the reader's own life*

- Post-reading Activities

- Book Report Ideas

- Research Ideas

- A Culminating Activity

- Three Different Options for Unit Tests

- Bibliography

- Answer Key

We are confident that this unit will be a valuable addition to your literature planning, and that as you use our ideas, your students will learn to treasure the stories to which you introduce them.

Sample Lesson Plan

Lesson 1

- Introduce and complete some or all of the pre-reading activities found on page 5.
- Read "About the Author" with your students. (page 6)
- Read book summary with students. (page 7)
- Introduce the vocabulary list for Section 1. (page 8)

Lesson 2

- Read Chapters 1 and 2. As you read, place the vocabulary words in the context of the story and discuss their meanings.
- Choose a vocabulary activity. (page 9)
- Complete "Taking Sides." (page 11)
- Learn to anticipate the story. (page 12)
- Discuss the book in terms of the Metropolitan Museum of Art. (page 13)
- Begin Readers' Response Journals. (page 14)
- Administer the Section 1 quiz. (page 10)
- Introduce the vocabulary list for Section 2. (page 8)

Lesson 3

- Read Chapters 3 and 4. Place the vocabulary words in context and discuss their meanings.
- Choose a vocabulary activity. (page 9)
- Establish a museum. (page 16)
- Learn to use a compass. (page 17)
- Discuss the book in terms of the history of the Italian Renaissance. (pages 18-19)
- Ask the students to describe what it means to be a team player. (page 20)
- Administer the Section 2 quiz. (page 15)
- Introduce the vocabulary list for Section 3. (page 8)

Lesson 4

- Read Chapters 5 and 6. Place the vocabulary words in context and discuss their meanings.
- Choose a vocabulary activity. (page 9)
- Design your own mark. (page 22)
- Have a group planning session. (page 23)
- Discuss the book in terms of a biography of Michelangelo. (page 24)
- Sculpt a statue. (page 25)
- Write about painting the Sistine Chapel ceiling. (page 26)

- Administer the Section 3 quiz. (page 21)
- Introduce the vocabulary list for Section 4. (page 8)

Lesson 5

- Read Chapters 7 and 8. Place the vocabulary words in context and discuss their meanings.
- Choose a vocabulary activity. (page 9)
- Build a model mastaba. (page 28)
- As a group, complete puzzle. (page 29)
- Discuss the book in terms of the United Nations. (page 30)
- Discuss individual differences. (page 31)
- Administer the Section 4 quiz. (page 27)
- Introduce vocabulary list for Section 6. (page 8)

Lesson 6

- Read Chapters 9 and 10. Place the vocabulary words in context and discuss their meanings.
- Choose a vocabulary activity. (page 9)
- Design a limousine. (page 33)
- Discuss the book in terms of point of view. (page 34)
- Complete "Adjective to Adverb." (page 35)
- Discuss the book in terms of changing viewpoints. (page 36)
- Administer the Section 5 quiz. (page 32)

Lesson 7

- Discuss questions about the story. (page 37)
- Assign book report and research projects. (pages 38 and 39)
- Begin work on the culminating activity. (pages 40, 41, and 42)

Lesson 8

- Administer Unit Test 1, 2, and/or 3. (pages 43, 44, and 45)
- Discuss the test answers and responses.
- Discuss the students' opinions and enjoyment of the book.
- Provide a list of related reading for students. (page 46)

Lesson 9

- Celebrate the "Festival of the Arts" culminating activity. (pages 40, 41, and 42)

Before the Book

Before reading *From the Mixed-up Files of Mrs. Basil E. Frankweiler,* it would be helpful for your students to have a feel for the setting of the book and to have some knowledge and appreciation of the art which plays such a large role in the story. In addition, try some of the following pre-reading activities to stimulate interest and help students focus on the literature.

1. Predict what the story might be about by hearing the title.

2. Predict what the story might be about by looking at the cover illustration.

3. Discuss other books by Elaine Konigsburg that students may have heard about or read.

4. Discuss anything the students already know about famous art and famous artists.

5. Discuss any museums the students may have visited.

6. Discuss anything the students may already know about New York City and the Metropolitan Museum of Art.

7. Show a book or a film about the Renaissance, and show the students pictures of some of the art which they will be reading about in *From the Mixed-up Files of Mrs. Basil E. Frankweiler.*

8. To give your students a feel for the time in which Michelangelo lived and worked and the significance of his art, read about Michelangelo and some of his contemporaries.

9. Discuss the students' ideas about the importance of art in the world today.

10. Visit an art museum.

11. Answer these questions:

    - Do you ever feel you're not appreciated at home?

    - Would you ever run away because you did not feel appreciated?

    - If you ran away, where would you go?

    - If you ran away, would you take your little brother?

    - What have you ever seen or heard about that interested you so much that you couldn't think of anything else until you learned more about it?

12. Write a description of the most beautiful thing you have ever seen. What was there about it that made it beautiful? Do you think that what seems beautiful to you is also beautiful to others? How can you tell?

About the Author

Although Elaine Lobl Konigsburg loved to read and draw as a child, it never occurred to her to become a writer until she was well into her adult years and had been a bookkeeper and a science teacher. Not even her closest college friends knew that she could write and draw, since she spent much of her college career filling long hours in the chemistry lab.

She left teaching shortly after the birth of her first child, and when she and her family moved to Port Chester, New York, she began exploring galleries, museums, and New York City. When her youngest child started school, she began writing, then reading what she'd written to her children to see their reactions.

Konigsburg made writing history in 1968 when her second book, *From the Mixed-up Files of Mrs. Basil E. Frankweiler,* won the Newberry award, and her first book, *Jennifer, Hecate, Macbeth, William McKinley, and Me* was the Newberry runner-up. Both of these books were illustrated as well as written by her. Her own children were the models for the children's pictures in the books.

Another book by Konisburg is *A Proud Taste for Scarlet and Miniver,* which is about Eleanor of Aquitaine, who lived during the twelfth century. Eleanor was what Konigsburg calls "a women's libber," because she had such a strong place in British history. She was the mother of two kings, Richard the Lion Heart and King John, who signed the Magna Carta in 1215. Eleanor established the rules for courtly love usually thought of in connection with King Arthur and his Knights of the Round Table.

Konigsburg usually spends between a year and a year-and-a-half writing a book. She writes and rewrites many times, and doesn't send it to the publisher until it's exactly the way she wants it to be. She believes that children's books need to have "a certain kind of excellence." While she wants them to appear nonchalant and easy, she also wants them to be based on good writing techniques and accurate history.

Konigsburg was born in New York, New York. She attended the Carnegie Institute of Technology (now Carnegie-Mellon University) and graduated with honors in 1952. She also did graduate study at the University of Pittsburgh and the Art Students' League. She is married to an industrial psychologist and is the mother of three children. Konigsburg has received many awards for her books, including the Newberry, Book World's Spring Book Festival, and the Lewis Carroll Shelf Award, among others. *From the Mixed-up Files of Mrs. Basil E. Frankweiler* was made into a movie starring Ingrid Bergman in 1973 and renamed *The Hideaways.* Another was made into a play, *The Second Mrs. Giaconda.*

Book Summary

(Available in USA, Dell; Canada, Doubleday Dell Seal; UK, Macmillan; AUS, Transworld Publishers)

Claudia was sick and tired of not being appreciated, so she decided to do the logical thing about her circumstances. She decided to run away. She knew just where she was going to go, too. There was only one problem. She didn't have much money, because she'd spent most of it on hot fudge sundaes. So she decided to ask her favorite little brother, Jamie, to go with her. Jamie had money, tons of it, which he'd won cheating at cards. Claudia figured that he certainly would have enough to pay for the most exciting adventure in the world.

Running away wasn't really hard at all. Claudia and Jamie packed their clean underwear in her violin case and his trumpet case. Then they took the train to New York, and established residence in the most beautiful place Claudia could think of, the Metropolitan Museum of Art.

What a place to hide out! It was full of wonderful things from all over the world: paintings, statues, armor from the middle ages, and a great fountain in which to bathe. They even had huge canopy beds to sleep in at night. However, that wasn't enough to hold Claudia's interest very long. But then the children discovered the lovely little angel, the most mysterious thing Claudia had ever seen. Who had carved it? Was it really carved by Michelangelo? Not even the experts seemed to know.

The statue had a magic which trapped Claudia, and she simply couldn't return home until she discovered its maker. And who was Mrs. Basil E. Frankweiler? How could she help Claudia solve the mystery so the children could go home?

Newbery Award-winning *From the Mixed-up Files of Mrs. Basil E. Frankweiler* is full of humor and suspense as Claudia and Jamie explore the museum and New York City, searching for the answer to the angel's mystery.

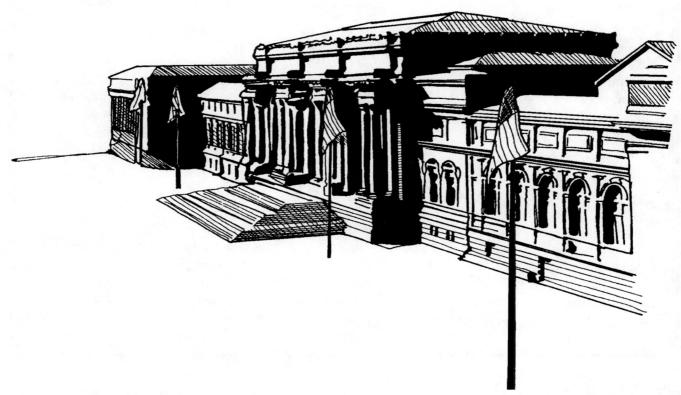

Vocabulary Lists

Section 1
(Chapters 1 and 2)

knapsack	suburbs	jostle	complement	temptation
penetrate	injustice	commute	specialize	transistor
obvious	tyranny	tycoon	pout	percolator
chain mail	stowaway	monotony	appreciation	pamphlet
forceps	complicate	Neanderthal	retrace	perspiration

Section 2
(Chapters 3 and 4)

curator	exhaustive	mediocre	condemn	exchequer
canopy	acquisition	embalm	impostor	conspicuous
chauffeur	commotion	ornate	perilous	urn
accumulate	carbon dioxide	mimic	intrigue	orthopedic
chancellor	elegant	Renaissance	tapestry	sarcophagus

Section 3
(Chapters 5 and 6)

executive	pagan	investigate	pedestal	telepathy
sprite	stonemason	authority	corporation	espresso
petit fours	stealthily	emblem	sawhorse	dismal
absolute	footnote	parentheses	corpuscle	embroider
conscience	diagram	associate	indicate	browse

Section 4
(Chapters 7 and 8)

solemn	stroll	derby	heroine	summarize
biographer	accomplish	sarcastic	consult	pharaoh
muzzle	patience	challenge	furnace	topaz
attribute	altar	cupid	calculate	mastaba
abrasion	sari	quarry	righteous	consensus

Section 5
(Chapters 9 and 10)

pauper	abrupt	baroque	peer	frantic
astound	muted	saunter	sonnet	analyze
receptions	antique	emit	chandelier	stammer
casserole	trance	coincidence	ascend	Oriental
fluorescence	theatrics	kaleidoscope	auction	circumstance
charity	categories	urgency	poll	

Vocabulary Activity Ideas

Completing some vocabulary activities based on the words in the book will help your students learn and retain the words. A list of vocabulary words is provided for each section of the book. You may use all of them, or choose words which are most appropriate for your students.

The students may work in small groups or individually to study the words. Here are a few ideas for activities to try with the vocabulary words in *From the Mixed-up Files of Mrs. Basil E. Frankweiler.*

- **Color My Word**

  In this activity students are to imagine what a word would look like if it had a shape and was a certain color. After using their imaginations, students can be encouraged to illustrate the word in the appropriate color.

- **Cross My Word**

  Make a crossword out of some of the vocabulary words. Number the first letter of each word. The students then write clues for the words based on their meanings.

- **Auction My Word!**

  Students are to choose a word they particularly like more than another. Then each student is to write a script telling why he/she likes using that word best and why others should use it too. Using his/her script as a guide, the student then tries to persuade the other students to "buy" his/her word. After all students have given their speeches, vote to see which is the most popular word. The word that gets the largest number of prospective buyers is declared the winner.

- **My Word, the Extraterrestrial**

  Each student is to choose a word and imagine that word to be an extraterrestrial. What would the word look like if it were from another world? Then have each student write a description of what the word looks like.

- **My Word, the Artist**

  Each student is to imagine a vocabulary word to be the name of a make-believe artist. What kind of pictures would that artist paint? Draw and color a picture in the style of that make-believe artist.

- **Word Categories**

  In groups, divide the words into categories based on whether each is a noun, verb, or adjective. Are any words left over? What category of words are left over? As a class, share each group's findings.

- **Make an Illustrated Dictionary**

  In small groups, students are to work together to create an illustrated dictionary of all or a selection of vocabulary words.

- **Write an Art History Lesson**

  Individually, or in small groups, students are to use vocabulary words to describe a particular period in the history of art.

Quiz Time

1. On the back of this paper list three significant events from Section 1.

2. Why did Claudia feel that she needed to run away?

   _____

   _____

3. What did Claudia like most about the idea of running away?

   _____

   _____

4. When did Claudia's "fiscal week" begin?

   _____

   _____

5. In well-written sentences, describe Claudia's plan for the runaway trip.

   _____

   _____

6. Why did Jamie have so much money?

   _____

   _____

7. Where did Claudia tell Jamie to hide his trumpet?

   _____

   _____

8. Why didn't the bus driver discover Claudia and Jamie hiding on the bus?

   _____

   _____

9. Why did Jamie make so much noise as he walked off the bus?

   _____

   _____

10. What was in the two letters that Claudia mailed when she and Jamie got off the train?

    _____

Taking Sides

When an event takes place, the people involved in the event each see it in a different way, don't they? For example, if there is an automobile accident, the driver who is at fault will see the accident in one way, the injured person in the other car will have another opinion about what happened, and someone else, who was standing on the corner nearby and observing the accident, may have an entirely new idea about what has occurred. We call this way of looking at the same thing differently "point of view."

How did Claudia and Jamie feel after they ran away from home? How do you think their parents felt when the children did not return home from school? In the box below on the left, draw or write any words or symbols which show how Claudia and Jamie felt. In the box on the right, draw or write any word or symbols which show how their parents felt.

Claudia and Jamie	**Their Parents**

Write a well-written paragraph which explains the meaning of the symbols and words you have chosen. Tell the point of view of Claudia and Jamie, and tell the point of view of their parents about the children's running away. How are they the same or different?

Anticipation Guide

Completing an **Anticipation Guide** prior to reading a book can help your students gain more meaning from their reading by helping them focus on the characters and events in the book.

Before beginning your reading of *From the Mixed-up Files of Mrs. Basil E. Frankweiler,* show the book to your students and tell them they are going to read it. Ask them to look closely at the book's cover illustration. Then separate them in small groups and ask them to take two minutes to predict what the book may be about.

Have each student complete the **Anticipation Guide.** Explain to the students that their answers will not be graded, and that they have a right to their opinions. Collect the **Anticipation Guides,** and discuss the answers with the class. Give the same questions to the class after the reading of the book is completed. Discuss any changes of opinions which have occurred after reading the book.

Anticipation Guide

Write **YES** if you agree with a statement, and write **NO** if you do not.

1. Only sissies are interested in painting, sculpture, and ballet.

   _____

2. A museum is not a place to go for fun.

   _____

3. Nothing exciting ever happens in a museum.

   _____

4. Most people are not creative.

   _____

5. Brothers and sisters just can't get along with each other.

   _____

The Metropolitan Museum of Art

Have you ever been to a large museum, such as the Metropolitan Museum of Art?

Located in New York City is the "Met." This is the largest art museum in the western hemisphere. It holds more than two million pieces of art from all over the world, including ones from ancient Egypt, Greece, and Rome, and its collection of European art is the largest in the world outside Europe.

In eighteen separate departments such works may be found as African and Oceanic art, Native North and South American art, medieval art and architecture, prints, drawings, photographs, costumes, musical instruments, and decorative arts from the Renaissance to the twentieth century. The American Wing's vast collection is the largest and most comprehensive in the world. A special branch of the museum, The Cloisters, contains art from the Middle Ages.

The Metropolitan Museum was founded in 1870 by a group of civic leaders, industrialists, and art collectors. It was moved to its present location in 1880. Its primary purpose is to acquire, preserve, and exhibit works from a wide variety of places and different times, and it serves as an educational facility by having regular exhibitions and programs for the public.

The museum also conducts many classes. There are gallery tours in English every day, as well as in Japanese, German, French, and Spanish on certain days.

Activity

Write a letter to the museum, asking for a schedule of exhibits which will be held during the summer. Send your letter and a self-addressed stamped envelope to:

> **The Metropolitan Museum of Art**
> 1000 5th Ave. (at 82nd Street)
> New York, New York 10028-0198

When your schedule arrives, compile a list of the exhibits you would like to attend. Create your own visiting schedule such as the example below.

Exhibit	Where	Time

Readers' Response Journals

There is a significant difference between the way in which a competent reader reads a story and the way in which a less able reader reads it. Good readers do not have to struggle with the words, which allows them the opportunity to "get into" the story. Less able readers who must struggle in the process of decoding words often do not enjoy or comprehend what is read.

Response journals can be one of the most effective tools you can use in your teaching of literature. Appropriately structured, and written in daily, the journals can help even your reluctant reader to "get into" the reading by personalizing it for him/her and making it relevant. You may discover that after journaling, students will be able to focus better on what they read, and topics related to the reading which come up in class can be discussed more effectively.

Try some of these ideas with your students:

- Tell the students that the purpose of the journals is to allow them to write about how they feel and think about what they read.

- Before the reading, provide the question to be answered, so that students will be able to focus their reading and give more thoughtful responses.

- Ask for a variety of responses, both written and graphic. Sometimes ask for responses comparing a character's feelings before and after an event to show cause and effect, or compare two characters to each other.

- Provide cultural and historical information which will help your students to better place characters and events into the story's setting, as well as help them to understand their significance.

- Ask journal questions which relate characters and events in the story to their own lives. Help them to compare what they read with life as they know it and to express their feelings about situations in the story which may be similar in some ways to situations they have experienced.

- Write positive comments in the journals, and only grade them for completeness and effort.

- Allow time for journal writing every day. If at all possible, keep journals in the classroom. This will ensure that they are always available when needed, and will give your students the message that their journals are deserving of special treatment.

Quiz Time!

1. On the back of this paper, list three important events from Section 2.

2. What did Jamie consult to determine the direction he and Claudia were taking?

   _____

3. When Claudia and Jamie were in the museum, what directions did Claudia give Jamie about hiding in the men's room?

   _____

4. In a well-written sentence, describe how Jamie had control over his big sister.

   _____

5. How did Claudia and Jamie become a team?

   _____

   _____

6. What historical event had supposedly happened in the big canopy bed where Jamie and Claudia slept?

   _____

   _____

7. Where did Claudia and Jamie hide their things?

   _____

8. What did Claudia decide they should do to take advantage of the time they were spending in the museum?

   _____

   _____

9. In a well-written sentence, describe how Claudia and Jamie toured the Egyptian wing.

   _____

   _____

10. On the back of this paper, describe the statue, and tell why Claudia was so curious about her.

Establish a Museum

A good museum, whatever its theme and whatever its size, can be fascinating. Many wonderful hours may be spent wandering through its collections of art, artifacts, and historical relics.

If you could establish a museum of your own, what type would it be? Before you decide, think of some things you would need to consider.

First of all, you would need to determine your theme. What kind of museum will you have? Will you emphasize art, like the Metropolitan? What kind of art? If space is limited, you might have to limit your collection to one type or one period—for example, Native American pottery or paintings of the Old West. You might choose to display photographs of the town in which you live or even family photographs for a family museum.

Museums are often established to memorialize a certain person, such as a former President or a famous movie star. You might concentrate on items from a period of history, such as the age of the dinosaurs or the American Civil War, anything which whets your interest enough so that you think others will be interested as well. If your museum is to be a history museum, you would include items which could have actually existed during a certain period and which illustrate how life was at that time.

Natural history museums are also very interesting. You could establish a plant museum or a museum built around a special interest of yours: butterflies, birds, flowers, or medicinal plants used by a certain group of people in history.

Activity

Construct a model museum which you think would be interesting to others. When you decide the type of museum you wish to establish, you will then need a box, such as a shoe box and various craft materials. These might include colored paper, foil, glue and scissors.

Research the theme which you have chosen for your museum, then assemble the materials you need. Inside the box, use them to make miniatures of items which fit your theme.

Using a Compass

For this activity you will need a compass for every three or four students. They may be purchased inexpensively at sporting goods stores, surplus stores, or may often be borrowed from the teacher resource center at your school.

Compasses were used beginning at least as early as 1088 A.D. by the Chinese, by Arabian merchants in 1200 A.D., and by the Vikings about half a century later. One of the first compasses consisted of a piece of lodestone (a magnetized piece of magnetite) which floated on a piece of cork in a bowl of water. This early compass was based on the same principle as the ones we use today, the principle of magnetism.

Earth is a magnet. It has a magnetic north pole and a magnetic south pole. A compass needle is also a magnet with opposite poles. Magnetism is an invisible force which flows through certain metals and makes them attract or repel each other. A magnet has two ends. One end is a south pole, and the other end is a north pole, just like the Earth. The opposite poles attract each other.

A compass needle lines up with the Earth's line of magnetic force, and this force always makes the compass needle point north. The needle spins on a very thin post. The compass is marked with the directions: north, south, east and west. Some compasses are complicated with specialized features for different uses, but students can easily learn how to use the basic compass.

To take an accurate bearing with a compass, follow these directions:

1. Face the object whose bearing you wish to find. Frame the compass between your thumbs and forefingers to form a triangle which points to the object.

2. Turn the compass until the north end of the needle points north on the dial.

3. Hold the compass still and read your bearing at the point where your forefingers touch.

Activity: In groups of three or four, have students take their bearings at several places in the classroom and on the school grounds. Record findings. Have each group share its findings with the class.

The Italian Renaissance

While he and Claudia were in the museum, Jamie decided that he wanted to learn about the Italian Renaissance, an exciting period of history, between the 14th and 16th centuries. Renaissance means rebirth, and the scholars and artists of the time saw what they were learning and creating as a rebirth of the glory of Rome and Greece. This feeling was particularly strong in Italy, the home of the Roman Empire centuries before.

When the Roman Empire collapsed, Europe entered a long era known as the Dark Ages. Learning and education declined and most people had to struggle very hard just to survive.

During the 14th century, however, governments gradually became secure enough that some people began to trade and accumulate wealth. As this happened, people began to want more for themselves than just a bit of food and a place to sleep. The excitement of the Renaissance occurred in the cities and towns which were much smaller than the ones today. There were no kings or countries as we know them. Naples, Milan, Florence, Venice, and the Papal States were controlled by the Pope, the head of the Church. The Pope was not just a leader of the Church; he also was a political ruler and occasionally became very powerful.

During the Renaissance many rulers who were interested in the arts became patrons who supported and encouraged artists to create paintings, sculpture, and architecture. These artists could then work without worrying about food or shelter. The most famous patron probably was Lorenzo de Medici, of Florence, who rebuilt St. Peter's Cathedral in Rome.

Things were very different then than they are today.

The quality of a person's everyday life depended upon which social class the person was born into. Most people were peasants or ordinary laborers who worked from sunrise to sundown. They would have Sundays and Saints' days off, but they were often at the mercy of soldiers or thieves who roamed the countryside looking for an easy penny or piece of food.

Medical care was poor. Half of the children died before their first birthdays. Many women died giving birth, and life expectancy was about thirty-five years. Hospitals served mainly to separate the sick from the well. Disease spread easily in the cities, where garbage was thrown into the streets, rats came out at night, and no sanitary facilities like bathrooms existed. Nothing was known about how disease was spread, and every few years the Plague wiped out one-third to one-half the population in a given town.

Despite the hardships and terrors, the arts and learning began to flourish. Scholars started to think again about the learning of the past, and artists began to portray the world more accurately than during the Dark Ages. They began to paint and sculpt bodies which looked real and question the world around them. Although only for boys, schools were begun and universities were founded.

The Italian Renaissance

(cont.)

When the Renaissance started, each book had to be laboriously copied by hand. Then Gutenburg invented a printing press. At first, most books appeared in Latin, the language of the Church, but were soon printed in the common language of the people.

At the same time, explorers were searching for truth in different ways, sailing around the world and proving that the world was not flat. New ways of conducting industry were invented. The human body was studied, clocks were made, and some of the world's greatest scholars and artists emerged.

One scholar was Galileo Galilei, sometimes called "the father of experimental science." He became a mathematician to earn a living but spent much time observing the heavens. He discovered that the earth and the planets moved around the sun, but powerful leaders of the Church insisted that the earth was the center of the universe. His writings were banned and he was sentenced to life in prison, but he continued to write until his sight failed him. He died in 1642.

Another scholar, Leonardo da Vinci, a great artist and genius saw with his mind's eye things that man had never before seen. He drew wonderful notebooks of fossils, muscles, plants, and eye structures. On paper he invented irrigation systems, pumps, cranes, diving helmets, and steam engines. He drew a helicopter, airplane, tank, and machine gun— altogether 5,000 pages of drawings with notes. This was more than 400 years before these things were actually made! His imagination and vision were far greater than anyone else's of his time. Leonardo's most famous painting is the *Mona Lisa*. The mysterious smile of the lady in the picture has intrigued all who have seen her. Another famous painting by Leonardo was *The Last Supper*, done with the newly invented oil paints.

Other artists also contributed to the Renaissance. Donatello and Michelangelo carved beautiful statues, and Ghiberti made the exquisite bronze doors for the baptistry in Florence. The lovely dome on the cathedral of Florence, designed by Brunelleschi, stands as a monument to the spirit of the age.

By 1650, the Renaissance was pretty much over, but many ideas from this great period enrich our lives today.

Activity: Imagine that there was to be a New Renaissance, a rebirth, today that would make a positive difference in your world. What would it be like? What do you think should change to make the world a better place? How would you be involved in this change? Draw a picture of the world as you see it now, and as it would be after the New Renaissance. Explain what you have drawn in writing and describe what you feel would be the best of all possible worlds.

Team Players

Claudia and Jamie became a team, a family of two. They had always been family, as long as they had been brother and sister, but this was different. Now, they felt like a team. They would still have arguments and disagreements, but the arguments would be discussions. Now, they would truly work together. The most important thing is that they really and truly cared for each other.

Have you ever been part of a team? Have you ever been so close to someone that you found yourselves working, or playing toward the same goal and really caring about each other? Maybe you have experienced this in a sports team, or a school club or group, or during an adventure you shared with a friend or with a brother or sister.

On the lines below, tell about an event which happened when you were part of a team. What did you do? How did it feel? What do you think is important for team members to do for each other? If you have never been part of a team, tell what you think it would be like and how you imagine it would feel.

_____

_____

_____

_____

_____

_____

_____

_____

_____

_____

_____

_____

_____

_____

_____

From the Mixed-up Files of Mrs. Basil E. Frankweiler

Quiz Time!

1. On the back of this paper, list three important events from Section 3.

2. Where did Claudia and Jamie go to work on the mystery of the angel?

_____

3. What task did Claudia assign to Jamie to do in their search?

_____

4. Which artist did some people believe had carved the angel?

_____

5. In a well-written sentence, describe how Jamie teased Claudia with a candy bar.

_____

_____

6. In a well-written sentence, describe the conversation Jamie heard in the men's room.

_____

_____

7. How did Claudia and Jamie get additional income? In your opinion was this act honest or dishonest?

_____

_____

8. What clue did Claudia and Jamie find on the pedestal?

_____

9. Where did they find the answer to the riddle about the mark on the bottom of the statue?

_____

_____

10. To whom did Claudia send a letter? What was the purpose of the letter?

_____

_____

Make Your Mark

Claudia and Jamie discovered that a mark had been left in relief (the projection of a figure from a flat background) on the velvet on which the angel had stood. Then they learned that the mark on the velvet was the stonemason's mark carved by Michelangelo on the bottom of his statues to identify them. The mark was three intersecting circles, one of which contained an M for Michelangelo. This mark became his mark, a symbol saying: This is the work of Michelangelo.

Today, people in business often design some sort of symbol to stand for their business or service, and they use this symbol on business cards, signs, and advertisements. We sometimes call this mark a "logo."

Imagine that you are an artist. You want to make certain that later you'll be able to prove that you created a statue. Design a mark to use on your work of art. In the box below, draw your mark.

Make Your Plan

Claudia thought a lot about how she and Jamie would spend their time in the Metropolitan, but she hadn't planned on their finding a puzzle which would intrigue them like the mystery of who carved the angel statue. After they found the mark on the velvet on which the statue had stood, they set out to find more clues and solve the mystery.

In groups of four or five, discuss the clues Claudia and Jamie found about the mark from the angel statue, and brainstorm your ideas about what they should do with the clues. Answer the following questions:

1. What clue did Claudia and Jamie find concerning the statue's origin?

   _____

   _____

2. What did they discover about that clue?

   _____

   _____

3. What did the children do with the information they discovered?

   _____

   _____

4. What do you predict may happen because of what the children are doing with the information they discovered?

   _____

   _____

5. Are they doing the right thing, or do you think they should devise another plan instead?

   _____

   _____

Return to your seats with this sheet and the answers your group has written. Write your own plan that you think Claudia and Jamie should follow with their revealing information.

Michelangelo

Before reading *From the Mixed-up Files of Mrs. Basil E. Frankweiler*, had you ever heard of Michelangelo? Michelangelo was one of the greatest artists the world has ever known. Born March 6, 1475, in Caprese, Italy, he and Leonardo da Vinci did much to cause the Italian Renaissance.

Michelangelo wanted to be an artist from his childhood. He grew up in the Settignano district—famous for its stone quarries—near Florence. It was here he probably learned to chisel stone. At that time an artist was considered only a day laborer, and his father was against his becoming an artist, so Michelangelo was sent to school. He did not do well in his studies, preferring to spend most of his time drawing. Finally, after many arguments with his father, Michelangelo was apprenticed to Domenico Ghirlandaio, a famous painter, from whom he learned to paint in fresco, a method of painting onto wet plaster.

About a year later, he was taken to visit the home of Lorenzo de Medici. Full of art and statues, the home was a center for art for the entire city of Florence. Once he saw the wonderful art treasures which filled the home and the grounds, Michelangelo never again returned to Ghirlandaio's.

Most art of the time was religious in nature, and so it was that Michelangelo's first really well-known sculpture was the *Pietá*, a statue of Mary holding the crucified Christ, which he carved for St. Peter's Church in Rome. In 1504 he completed his statue of *David*. Over 12 feet (3.6 m) high, this statue had the power and strength of the best Greek sculpture. Michelangelo was commissioned to work for at least seven different Popes.

Probably the greatest of Michelangelo's creations is the ceiling of the Sistine Chapel, which took four years to paint. Michelangelo had not wanted to paint the ceiling, wanting to sculpt instead, but Pope Julius II insisted. Once he had agreed to do it, he determined that it would be a work of art unmatched by any other. The ceiling measured 40 feet by 130 feet (12 m x 39 m), and its center curved up to more than 60 feet (18 m) above the floor. At times lying on his back on a scaffold he had designed, he worked on the ceiling and finished it in October, 1512. With scenes from the Bible painted in fresco, the ceiling is truly one of the world's wonders in art. Twenty-nine years after he completed the ceiling, he also painted *The Last Judgement* on the altar wall of the chapel. He continued creating art until he died at the age of 88.

Michelangelo *(cont.)*

Michelangelo's first success as a sculptor came early in his life when he carved a life-sized statue of the wine god Bacchus. At the age of twenty-three he carved a version of the traditional *Pietá*, which portrays a mourning Mary holding Jesus. This larger-than-life statue established Michelangelo. The statue is now housed in St. Peter's Basilica in Rome.

What is it like to be a sculptor? How does it feel to create a statue. To gain a greater appreciation for the work of Michelangelo, try this simple sculpting activity.

Materials:

- bar of soap or piece of clay
- small toy animal or angel about the same size as the soap or clay
- carving tools—butter knives, cheese spreaders, toothpicks
- pencil
- container of water

Directions:

Choose a simple animal or angel to sculpt. The lines should be very simple to copy. Study the shape of the object by both looking closely at it and holding it in your hand. Turn it over so you can see how it is made. Place it nearby where it is clearly visible.

Take the soap or clay and study it. Determine where you will begin your sculpting. Use the tip of a carving tool or a pencil and outline the areas you wish to carve away.

Cut into the soap or clay. Take your time, carving out small pieces first. If you need to soften the soap to make it easier to manipulate, use a small amount of water on it. When you have finished the outline, use whatever carving tools you can to create a smooth finish for your project. If you have never carved before, you may find this hard to do, so be patient.

Display it next to the animal or angel you attempted to copy.

Painting the Ceiling

Michelangelo did not want to paint the ceiling of the Sistine Chapel. He was a sculptor, not a painter. But Pope Julius II was powerful, and if he wanted something done, it had to be done. So Michelangelo surveyed what was to become his canvas for more than four years. It was huge—40' by 130' (12 m x 39 m), shaped like a barn, with its center more than sixty feet (18 m) in the air. He didn't like the subject matter the Pope chose—the twelve apostles—and the physical problems of constructing a scaffold on which to work and of dealing with mold which appeared in the wet plaster were enormous. But once he managed to get the Pope to let him change the subject matter, he was determined to create the most magnificent painting ever done.

Imagine you are Michelangelo. In the circle on the left, place words and symbols which show how you feel before painting the ceiling. In the circle on the right, place words and symbols which show how you feel when you've finished painting the ceiling.

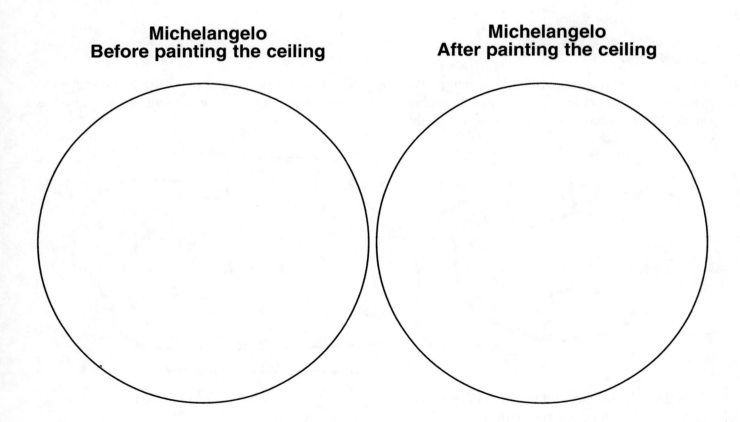

**Michelangelo
Before painting the ceiling**

**Michelangelo
After painting the ceiling**

Still imagining that you are Michelangelo, write an autobiographical account which tells how you feel when you first begin painting the ceiling and how you feel after you have finished it. What changes have taken place? How has the four years of painting, sometimes lying on your back, or standing high on a scaffold leaning backward to paint above your head, changed your life? Was what you have accomplished worth the work and trouble?

Quiz Time!

1. On the back of this paper list three important events from Section 4.

2. What event led Claudia to say to Jamie, "We'll take a long, long bath tonight."?

   _____

   _____

3. Who were the surprise visitors at the mastaba in the museum?

   _____

4. Where did Jamie deliver the letter?

   _____

5. In several well-written sentences, tell the story Jamie gave the tour guide at the U.N. about why they weren't in school.

   _____

   _____

6. Why was Claudia intrigued by the tour guide?

   _____

   _____

7. What did Claudia decide she was going to do when she was grown?

   _____

8. Why was it possible that the statue had not been carved by Michelangelo, even though his mark was on the bottom?

   _____

   _____

9. After Claudia and Jamie read the letter from the museum, what did Claudia do?

   _____

   _____

10. On the back of this paper, tell why Claudia and Jamie decided to go to Farmington instead of their home in Greenwich.

Build a Mastaba

Claudia and Jamie went to the Egyptian wing of the Metropolitan to look for their "group of the day." Deciding to look the group over before joining it, they went into a reconstructed tomb, from which they would be able to observe the class. The tomb they hid in was called a mastaba.

Built during the time in Egypt's history called the Old Kingdom, a mastaba was shaped somewhat differently than the pyramid tombs with which you may be familiar. It was oblong with walls that slanted slightly toward the center of the building toward flat roofs. The earliest mastaba may have been intended to look like a house, for mastabas were built of brick in the shape of Egyptian houses of that time.

In about the year 2700 B.C., a type of tomb called the Step Pyramid was built in Saqqara. This tomb looked like six mastabas piled on top of each other with each a little smaller than the one directly below it. The Pharaoh Djoser was buried in this type of tomb. All the pyramids which we call "the great pyramids," including those at Giza, were built within 400 years following the building of the Step Pyramid.

Activity

Build a model mastaba of your own using materials which are easily available to you. You could use LEGOs, sugar cubes, or make small bricks of clay to construct your model.

To make bricks you will need:

- "pattern" for brick made from soap, soft wood, or clay
- liquid latex obtained from a hobby store
- soap solution of 1 teaspoon (5 mL) liquid detergent to 1 cup (250 mL) water
- casting plaster from a hobby store or plaster of paris
- plywood or cardboard for base

Directions:

1. Determine the approximate number of bricks you will need.
2. Cover pattern brick with several coats of latex to form a mold. Allow latex to dry, then remove pattern brick.
3. Dip mold into detergent solution; wipe lightly.
4. Preparing only as much as you need for two or three bricks, prepare plaster according to package directions. Work quickly, because plaster cannot be thinned once it begins to set.
5. Pour plaster into mold, working it into crevices with a toothpick. Allow it to set for 15 to 30 minutes.
6. Remove brick from mold and allow it to dry for a day or longer.
7. Repeat process until you have the number of bricks you need.

Renaissance Crossword

In small groups, go to the library and research to discover the answers needed to complete the puzzle.

Across

4. Wrote *The Price*
7. Venetian who painted *Bacchus and Ariane*
8. Most famous German Renaissance figures painter
9. Designed the dome for the Cathedral of Florence
12. First Bible printed from movable type
13. Painted three large scenes called *The Battle of San Romano*

Down

1. Painted the *Mona Lisa*
2. Model for *The Prince*
3. First Italian painter to paint realistic figures
4. Carved marble and painted the ceiling of the Sistine Chapel
5. Polish astronomer who suggested that the sun was the center of the universe
6. Started the Protestant Reformation
8. Created a bronze statue of *David*
10. Known for his many paintings of the Madonna and Child
11. One of the most influential humanist thinkers of the Renaissance

The United Nations

When Claudia and Jamie visited the United Nations in New York City, they went to a place which is a center filled with the art of many nations, but it is much more than a museum. At the U.N., history, which affects the entire world, is made every day.

In 1945, when the long and bloody World War II finally came to an end, people of many countries saw a need for an international organization that could deal with the frequent crises between nations which could grow into widespread wars. One organization, the League of Nations, had already tried to do this, but it was a weak group and fell apart after a few years. The time was right for another attempt at peace. The people of the world were truly tired of war. Delegates from fifty countries signed the U.N.'s Charter at its first meeting in San Francisco. Now, the representatives of more than one hundred fifty countries are members of the U.N., and their central goal is peace and security for the world.

There are six main organs in the U.N.: the General Assembly, the Security Council, the Economic and Social Council, the Trusteeship Council, the International Court of Justice, and the Secretariat. All of these bodies are based in New York City at United Nations Headquarters, except for the Court, which is located at The Hague in the Netherlands. The money to purchase the sixteen acres on which the U.N. stands was donated by John D. Rockefeller, Jr. New York City gave some additional land and also contributed some improvements in the area. Although the U.N. is within the borders of the United States, it is legally international territory.

Today the U.N. plays such an important role in world affairs, it's difficult to imagine a world without it. The General Assembly deals with many worldwide concerns: war and peace, world economic problems, basic human rights, and potential benefits of scientific and technological advances. The Security Council is primarily concerned with maintaining international peace. Its five permanent members are China, France, Russia, the United Kingdom, and the United States. This is the body whose peacekeeping forces are sometimes sent to various trouble spots in the world. The Economic and Social Council attempts to achieve better standards of life and the promotion of human rights for all peoples. The goal of the Trusteeship Council is to help former colonial territories achieve independence and self government. The Secretariat is a body of people from over 150 nations in the world and includes experts from many different fields, (e.g., linguistics, economics, social science, the law, and administration) who prepare the reports and studies requested by the other branches of the U.N.

Activity: Find an article in the newspaper which concerns a current U.N. activity, and bring it to share with classmates.

The Unique You

Growing up has never been easy, and the age at which Claudia finds herself is one of the hardest times of all for young people. One's body is changing rapidly, the demands by family and friends are increasing, peer pressure to go along with the crowd is strong, and teachers seem to expect more all the time in terms of taking responsibility for completing assignments and for behavior. It is easy to look upon the good old days of childhood with longing, and it is also tempting to feel at times that no one appreciates us.

This is the mood in which Claudia has found herself and is the motive behind her decision to run away to the museum. Have you ever found yourself thinking that no one appreciates you? Most young people have. Fortunately, the feeling usually goes away in time and is replaced by a new determination to be the best one can be. Still, during adolescence, it is common to have changing feelings about yourself as you learn to adapt to your surroundings. Who are you today? Complete the following sentences, then without looking back to see what you answered the first time, repeat the exercise after a year's time. You will be amazed at how you have grown!

The Real Me—Today

Date _____   *My name* _____

1. If I could change my name, I would change it to _____

2. The color I like best is _____

3. When I watch television, I like to watch _____

4. My favorite music is _____

5. My best friend is_____, but I also like_____and
   _____ a lot.

6. When I have free time, I like to _____

7. I like to eat _____ more than anything else.

8. My favorite book is _____, and my favorite movie is_____

9. When I finish school I want to be _____

10. The hardest thing for me in school is _____

11. I am afraid of _____

12. I really get angry when _____

13. If I could have three wishes, I would want _____

On the back of this paper, draw a self-portrait of yourself.

Quiz Time!

1. On the back of this paper, list three important events from Section 5.

2. What did Jamie call Mrs. Frankweiler's house when he first saw it?

   _____

   _____

3. When asked, what did Jamie say was the nature of his and Claudia's business?

   _____

   _____

4. Describe the inside of Mrs. Basil E. Frankweiler's house.

   _____

   _____

5. Compare the way Claudia "cleaned up" for lunch with the way Jamie did.

   _____

   _____

6. In a well-written sentence, describe the secret Jamie accidentally divulged to Mrs. Frankweiler.

   _____

   _____

7. What did Claudia consider to be the most fun part of running away?

   _____

8. In a well-written sentence, describe Mrs. Frankweiler's method for allowing Claudia and Jamie an opportunity to discover the secret of the angel.

   _____

   _____

9. What was the secret?

   _____

   _____

10. Why did Mrs. Frankweiler not sell the sketch?

    _____

    _____

Order Your Custom-made Limo!

Claudia and Jamie are finally on their way home, and what a way to go—in a real limousine, not a rented one, but a private one—the one that belongs to Mrs. Basil E. Frankweiler, a Rolls Royce with everything!

Now, picture this! You have just become the heir to a very large fortune. For the first time in your life, you can have anything you wish to have. One of the things you have always wanted is a real limo of your own. You can just see the eyes of your classmates as you drive up to the front of the school in the classiest limo ever built, and it is all yours! In fact, the manufacturer built this spectacular car to order for you and spent much time in ensuring that every little detail was produced just exactly as you wanted it.

On the order blank below, show all of the features of your fantastic limousine for the car maker of your choice.

Name _____ Date _____

Auto company name _____

Name of limo _____

      Color(s) _____

      Length _____

      Interior color _____

Special features requested (Be specific about what needs you have; give reasons.)

_____

_____

_____

_____

_____

Date by which you need to take possession of limo _____

Means of payment _____

                           Signed _____

Point of View

Stories are always told from the angle or perspective of a certain person in that story. That position is called **point of view**. Behind every point of view is, of course, the author. Sometimes the author tells the events in a story, shifting perspective from time to time and making comments on what is happening. He or she may reveal an attitude toward what is happening in the story and may focus on the main character, telling the story through that character, but he or she does not write as though he or she is the main character. This point of view is called the **omniscient** point of view.

Sometimes the author tells the story in the **first person** point of view. In this point of view, a narrator tells the story as either a participant in the story or as a personal observer of it. He or she may or may not be the main character.

Occasionally, the point of view in a story may shift from one character to another. Many authors do not like to write a story in this way, because it can be confusing to the reader, as well as being more difficult to write than a story told from only one point of view.

Activity

From whose point of view is *From The Mixed-up Files of Mrs. Basil E. Frankweiler* told? Is it told from Mrs. Frankweiler's point of view? Is it told from Claudia's point of view? Or is the story told from the point of view of someone standing on the outside?

In groups of four or five, discuss these questions. Using examples of description or dialogue from the book, list reasons to show that the story is told from a certain point of view, and make your final decision based on what you believe to be the best reasons. Bring your decision back to share with the rest of the class.

Mrs. Frankweiler	Claudia	Someone Outside

Adjective to Adverb

When Claudia said, "I didn't say differently, I said different. I want to go back different," she showed that she knew how to use adjectives and adverbs correctly. If she had said, "I want to go back differently," she would have been saying she wanted to return by a different route or in a different mode of transportation. But that wasn't what she wanted to say. She wanted to say that when she went home she wanted to be different than she had been when she left.

Sometimes people have trouble telling the difference between adjectives and adverbs. With words like "different" and "differently," how can you know which is the correct one to use? In order to know which word to use, we need to review what **adjectives** and **adverbs** are.

Adjectives are words that describe a person, place, or thing.

Adverbs are words that modify, or change, verbs, adjectives, or other adverbs. Adverbs usually tell how. For example, in "drive slowly," slowly is an adverb which tells how the driving will or should be done. It modifies the verb "drive." In "very tall," very is an adverb which tells how tall something is. It modifies an adjective. Many adverbs end in "ly," but be careful not to assume that every word ending in "ly" is an adverb. It may be, but there are exceptions. "Lovely" ends in "ly," but it is an adjective, because it describes a noun.

Activity: Below is a list of adjective and adverb pairs. Write a sentence for each word to demonstrate the correct usage of each. Share your sentences with the class.

careful: _____ _____ _____	large: _____ _____ _____
carefully: _____ _____ _____	largely: _____ _____ _____
happy: _____ _____ _____	quiet: _____ _____ _____
happily: _____ _____ _____	quietly: _____ _____ _____

Changing Viewpoints

In chapter 10 of *From the Mixed-up Files of Mrs. Basil E. Frankweiler,* we are told about Claudia and Jamie's trip home in Mrs. Frankweiler's limousine. The person telling the story is the chauffeur, Sheldon. He tells a segment of the story as though he were a bystander watching.

In this activity, you are going to rewrite the trip home by changing the point of view. So far, we have known only as much of what Jamie has thought or felt, as Mrs. Frankweiler, Sheldon, or Claudia has allowed us to. Now, imagine that you are Jamie. On the lines below, rewrite the account of the trip home from your point of view. What were you thinking and feeling in the limousine, and how did Claudia and Sheldon appear to you? If you need more room, continue writing on the other side of this page.

_____

_____

_____

_____

_____

_____

_____

_____

_____

_____

_____

_____

_____

_____

_____

_____

Any Questions?

When you finished reading *From the Mixed-up Files of Mrs. Basil E. Frankweiler*, did you have some questions that were left unanswered? Write some of your questions here.

_____

_____

_____

Work in groups or by yourself to prepare possible answers for some or all of the questions you have asked above and those written below. When you have finished your predictions, share your ideas with the class.

- What happens to Claudia when she gets back to school? Does anyone at school know about where she has been? Does Claudia tell the class about what she learned about Michelangelo? Does she go on to learn more about da Vinci and other important people in the Italian Renaissance?

- What happens to Claudia and Jamie when they return home? Were their parents angry? Had their brothers been afraid? Were they grounded or put on restriction? Did Claudia manage to tell her parents that she felt unappreciated? Did Claudia and Jamie ever go on another adventure? If they did, where did they go? Did their parents start showing more appreciation for Claudia after she returned home?

- Did Mrs. Frankweiler ever tell her secret about Angel? When Mrs. Frankweiler died, did Claudia and Jamie inherit the sketch? Did they keep it, or did they sell it? Were experts able to prove that both the sketch and the statue were authentic? How old did Mrs. Frankweiler get to be before she died? Did she have any family? What did she do with her home? Did she leave it to the museum? How did Parks and Sheldon earn their livings after Mrs. Frankweiler's death?

- Was it hard for Claudia and Jamie to get back to "normal" after their adventure? Did school still seem like the same old thing, or had it now become comforting in its sameness? What did Claudia do the next time she felt unappreciated? Did she think of something to do instead of running away?

- What did the police do when Claudia and Jamie returned home? Were there any charges filed against them? Did the bus driver get in trouble for not checking the back seat of the bus? Was security at the museum increased after officials learned about Claudia and Jamie staying there for a week? What did the newspapers and television newscasts, which had reported the children's disappearance, report after they returned home?

- Did Mr. and Mrs. Kincaid become stricter as a result of the runaway? How did Claudia and Jamie explain their adventure to their little brothers? Did the brothers ever try to do what Claudia and Jamie did?

Book Report Ideas

There are many ways to report on a book once it has been read. After you finish reading *From the Mixed-up Files of Mrs. Basil E. Frankweiler,* choose a method of your own, or one of the suggestions below.

- **Create an Art Book**

  Use your own tastes in art to help you create a book on art. Your book can be one which is entirely about the art of one artist whose work you particularly enjoy. Or it could be about a "school" of art which interests you, such as impressionism, Cubism, or the Dutch school. It might be about one form of art, such as sculpture, watercolors, or architecture. It will be easier for you to create your own book if you limit it to one field or one artist. There are so many wonderful artists creating in so many different ways, it would be impossible to cover them all.

- **Paint a Picture**

  Using waterpaints, oils, or acrylics, paint a picture of a scene in *From the Mixed-up Files of Mrs. Basil E. Frankweiler.* This might be your interpretation of one of the art objects mentioned in the book. For example, you might paint a picture of Claudia and Jamie looking at the Angel, or the long line of people waiting to see it.

- **Sculpt a Statue**

  Lucky you, if you are able to sculpt! If you are, use your talent to make a statue Claudia and Jamie might have found in the museum.

- **Write a Biography**

  Choose an artist whose work is exhibited in the Metropolitan Museum of Art, and write a biography of that artist. Research the artist in the library, make your finished work into a book, and illustrate it in an appropriate way for that artist.

- **Conduct an Interview**

  With another student, conduct an interview in which one of you portrays the artist and the other portrays a newspaper reporter for the Sunday art pages of a local newspaper. Write and ask thoughtful questions requiring thoughtful answers. Then turn the interview into an article. At the beginning of your article, be sure to include a paragraph which contains the "five W's" of reporting: who, what, where, when, and why (or how).

- **Compare and Contrast**

  Write a paper in which you compare and contrast two entirely different types of art, such as the Romantic Movement and Impressionism, or the works of Michelangelo and those of Van Gogh. Remember, when you compare, you tell how things are the same, and when you contrast, you tell how things are different.

- **Make an illustrated map** of the Metropolitan Museum of Art.

Research Ideas

Describe three things in *From the Mixed-up Files of Mrs. Basil E. Frankweiler* that you would like to learn more about.

1. _____

2. _____

3 _____

While reading *From the Mixed-up Files of Mrs. Basil E. Frankweiler* you have encountered many names, artists, and ideas which may be very new to you. Knowing more about the people and places mentioned in the book will help you to have a better understanding of it and will increase your enjoyment of E.L. Konigsburg's ability as a writer.

Work in groups or alone to research one of the areas you named above or the areas listed below. Choose any oral presentation format you wish to share your findings with the rest of the class.

- Cave paintings
- Ancient Greek art
- Gothic stained glass
- Baroque art
- Impressionism
- Abstract art
- Ceramics
- Rubens
- El Greco
- Monet
- Metropolitan Museum of Art
- Museum of Modern Art
- Remington
- Architecture
- Egyptian art
- Pottery of Crete
- The Bayeux Tapestry
- English Renaissance
- The Romantic School
- Expressionism
- Greek sculpture
- da Vinci
- Goya
- Manet
- American Art
- National Gallery, London
- Western artists
- British Museum
- Islamic art
- Paintings of Crete

- Byzantine art
- Italian Renaissance
- Spanish artists
- Pointillism
- Modern sculpture
- Michelangelo
- Velasquez
- Constable
- Dali
- Tate Gallery, London
- Smithsonian Institute
- The Louvre, Paris
- Medieval art
- Egyptian tomb paintings
- Ancient Roman art
- Early Christian art
- The Utrecht School
- Post-Impressionists
- Fantasy
- Oriental art
- Rembrandt
- Turner
- Renoir
- National Gallery, Washington, D.C.
- Museum of Fine Arts, Boston
- Prado, Madrid
- Art in film
- French art

Festival of the Arts

After finishing a good book, the reader feels many things: satisfaction at having made a new literary friend; a heightened interest in times, places, and people mentioned in the book; and a desire to celebrate the accomplishment in some way. Because most of the setting of *From the Mixed-up Files of Mrs. Basil E. Frankweiler* is in a museum and much of the action centers around an art object, what better way to celebrate the reading of the book than with a Festival of the Arts?

Because Claudia loved to plan and she enjoyed art, she would probably enjoy being the planner for the festival. But since Claudia isn't here, the class will need to choose the planners.

There are many things to decide: what displays and events to include; what food to serve, if any; who is responsible for what; who to invite; and, very important for an arts festival, what will be its theme? Will all student art be included? Or will the art displayed be limited to the type of art talked about in the book? Will "arts" be limited to visual arts (painting, drawing, sculpture), or will you also have exhibits of other art forms?

The place to start is with a brainstorming session. Divide into groups of four to six. Choose one person as the chairman and spokesperson and one as recorder. Together discuss the questions above, as well as any others you may have. List your ideas on the brainstorm sheet found on page 41. Then come back together as a class and vote on the major suggestions. In your deliberations, one food you might consider is Nouilles et fromage en casserole, which is what Mrs. Frankweiler served Claudia and Jamie for lunch. A recipe for this favorite lunchtime fare is on page 42. Suggestions for displays and events are found below.

Don't forget to make invitations. Why not have a classroom contest for the best design of an invitation? The invitation chosen could be copied for use by everyone. Or, you might choose to make individual invitations. Whichever you choose, roll the finished invitations and tie with a colorful piece of ribbon or yarn. And plan to have fun!

Exhibits

- Invitations submitted in contest
- Class journals
- Model museums
- Illustrated histories of the Italian Renaissance
- Personal marks
- Sculpture
- Posters of Renaissance art
- Models of mastabas
- Self-portraits
- Art from around the world

Events

- Contest for best invitation
- Lunch of Nouilles et fromage en casserole
- Demonstration on how to use a compass
- Oral presentation about art during the Renaissance
- Oral presentation of reports about individual artists or scientists of the Renaissance
- Demonstration of how Michelangelo painted the Sistine Chapel ceiling
- Talk by a guest artist
- Exhibit of art books

Arts Festival *(cont.)*

Each group should have a copy of this page to use for the brainstorming activity described on page 40.

Brainstorm Sheet

Title for the day

_____

_____

_____

Guests

_____

_____

_____

Events

_____

_____

_____

Exhibits

_____

_____

_____

What needs to be done?

_____

_____

_____

Order of events

_____

_____

_____

A Dish by Any Other Name

There is something about putting a French name onto a food which makes it sound special. Maybe that is because the French are known for preparing wonderfully rich and flavorful dishes, but it is also because there is something intriguing about the French language. Almost any food named in French words sounds exotic and mysterious, and giving a French name to something ordinary causes it to sound extraordinary.

Claudia was very interested in having Nouilles et fromage en casserole. And it is so very good to eat! Try this luncheon menu to go with it. The Nouilles et fromage en casserole may be made at home, brought to school, and kept warm on an electric warming tray. Raw vegetables and apples may be brought to school and kept cold and crisp in a picnic cooler.

Before beginning, remember to follow kitchen safety rules.

Menu

Nouilles et fromage en casserole
Carrot and celery sticks
Fresh apples and peanut butter
Milk or juice

Recipe for Nouilles et fromage en casserole

Ingredients: 1½ cups macaroni (375 mL)

3 tablespoons margarine or butter (45 mL)

3 tablespoons white flour (45 mL)

2 cups milk (500 mL)

¼ teaspoon salt (1.25 mL)

Pepper, if desired

2 cups shredded cheddar cheese (500 mL)

Dash of paprika or parsley

Directions: Cook macaroni in salted water until tender but not soggy; drain. Melt butter and blend with flour until moistened. Add milk. Cook, stirring until thick. Add cheese and stir until melted. Do not boil. Combine sauce and macaroni; stir until all macaroni is coated with cheese. Pour into 1 ½ quart (1500 mL) casserole dish and sprinkle with minced parsley or paprika. Bake at 350 degrees Fahrenheit (180 degrees Celsius) until bubbly and browned. Makes 6 to 8 servings.

Apples with Peanut Butter

Directions: Wash and cut apples into halves. Spread with either smooth or crunchy peanut butter.

Objective Test and Essay

Matching: Match the description of each character with his/her name.

1. _____ Sheldon   a. wore a beautiful sari

2. _____ Jamie   b. Claudia and Jamie's grandfather

3. _____ Bruce Lansing   c. Mrs. Frankweiler's chauffeur

4. _____ Claudia   d. sold a statue for $225

5. _____ Indian guide   e. was a tightwad

6. _____ Mrs. Frankweiler   f. Jamie used his name once

7. _____ Parks   g. Did he or didn't he create the angel?

8. _____ Saxonburg   h. was the center of a controversy

9. _____ Angel   i. the butler

10. _____ Michelangelo   j. liked secrets and enjoyed planning adventures

True or False: Answer true or false in the blanks below.

1. _____ Mrs. Frankweiler donated much art to the Metropolitan Museum of Art.

2. _____ Jamie won money by cheating at cards.

3. _____ Once planning it was over, Claudia quickly tired of an adventure.

4. _____ Claudia and Jamie became very fond of each other during their adventure.

5. _____ Jamie's first choice for something to study at the museum was the Italian Renaissance.

Short Answer: Write a brief response to each question in the space provided.

1. Where was Claudia and Jamie's home? _____

2. What did Claudia and Mrs. Frankweiler both love? _____

3. How did Claudia and Jamie keep clean in the museum? _____

4. In what city is the Metropolitan Museum of Art? _____

5. Who carved the angel? _____

Essay: Respond to the following on the back of this paper.

Until Claudia and Jamie left on their adventure, they had lived their lives much like any other brother and sister, in separate bedrooms, in the same house, with different friends, and coming together at mealtimes, but seeing the world from very different perspectives. But something happened during their adventure; they became a team. Explain how the two became a team, giving examples of how they worked together and showing how their feelings toward each other changed.

Essay Challenge: Include your definition of "team" in your essay.

Response Unit Test

Explain the meaning of these quotations in *From the Mixed-up Files of Mrs. Basil E. Frankweiler.*

Note to the teacher: Choose the appropriate number of quotes to which your students should respond.

Chapter 1   *She intended to return home after everyone had learned a lesson in Claudia appreciation.*

'Two cents for every card I have more than he has and five cents for every ace.'

Chapter 2   *'What did you expect him to pay me in? Traveler's checks?'*

Jamie spent seven of the twenty-eight-and-a-half railroad miles trying to convince his sister that they should try hiding in Central Park.

Chapter 3   *'We have no more allowance. No more income. You can't be extravagant any longer.'*

No one thought it strange that a boy and a girl, each carrying a book bag and an instrument case who would normally be in school, were visiting a museum.

Chapter 4   *Manning their stations, meant climbing back into the booths and waiting during the perilous time when the museum was open to staff, but not to visitors.*

As Claudia passed by, she thought that the angel was the most beautiful, most graceful little statue she had ever seen.

Chapter 5   *She assigned to Jamie the task of looking through the books and photographs of Michelangelo's work to find pictures of Angel.*

'It's delicious. Want a bite?'

Chapter 6   *'The rings the beer cans made would have crushed the plush of the velvet down. . . and the plush of this velvet is crushed up.'*

Chapter 7   *The 'come-on-boys' voice belonged to Miss Clendennan, Jamie's third grade teacher.*

Chapter 8   *'The boiler on the furnace broke. No heat. They had to dismiss school. You should have heard the explosion!'*

Chapter 9   *'Another museum.'*

Chapter 10   *'The boy, madam, spent the first five minutes of the trip pushing every button in the back seat.'*

Conversations

Work in size-appropriate groups to write and perform the conversations that might have occurred in one of the following situations. If you prefer, you may use your own conversation ideas for characters in *From the Mixed-up Files of Mrs. Basil E. Frankweiler.*

- As an adult, Claudia tells her daughter about Angel. *(2 persons)*

- Jamie tells Bruce how he always wins at cards. *(2 persons)*

- Mr. and Mrs. Kincaid meet Claudia and Jamie at the door when they return home. *(4 persons)*

- As adults, Jamie and Claudia discuss their adventure. *(2 persons)*

- Mrs. Frankweiler and Saxonburg discuss the way Claudia went about solving the mystery. *(2 persons)*

- In the future, Claudia's young daughter returns home after spending a week in the Museum of Modern Art with her little brother. *(2 persons)*

- Claudia gives an oral report on her adventure, and the class questions her about Angel. *(3-5 persons)*

- Mrs. Frankweiler and the Kincaids get together for a family dinner. *(6 persons)*

- Claudia and Jamie tell their little brother about bathing in the fountain. *(3 persons)*

- Mrs. Kincaid and Claudia have a serious discussion about Claudia's running away. *(2 persons)*

- The security guard catches Jamie hiding in the men's room, and Jamie tries to talk his way out of trouble. *(2 persons)*

- Jamie stumbles out onto the museum floor right in front of Miss Clendennan. *(2 persons)*

- Claudia tells the librarian what she is looking for, and the librarian helps her find the books which hold the secret to Angel. *(2 persons)*

- When Sheldon returns to Mrs. Frankweiler's house, he tells Parks, the butler, about the children's conversation in the limousine. *(2 persons)*

- Mr. and Mrs. Kincaid discuss their childrens' adventure. *(2 persons)*

- Newspaper reporters interview Mrs. Frankweiler about Angel. *(3-4 persons)*

- The writer who is writing Mrs. Frankweiler's biography learns that Claudia and Jamie know the secret about Angel and interviews Mrs. Frankweiler about it. *(2 persons)*

- The Chief Security Guard at the Metropolitan Museum of Art tells his staff that from now on there will be new security measures taken at the museum because of Claudia and Jamie's stay there. *(2-4 persons)*

- The Chief of School Transportation discusses new security measures on school buses with the school bus drivers. *(3-4 persons)*

Bibliography

Research and Resource

Brown, Christopher. *Rembrandt.* Rizzoli International Publications, Inc., 1979.

Butterworth, Brent and Lee Green. *The Big Book of How Things Work.* Publications International, LTD., 1991.

Cohen, B. Bernard. *Writing About Literature.* Scott Foresman and Company, 1963.

Cole, Bruce and Gealt, Adelheid. *Art of the Western World.* Summit Books, 1989.

Galyean, Beverly-Colleene. *Mind-Sight: Learning Through Imaging.* Center for Integrated Learning, 1983.

Goodenough, Simon. *The Renaissance: The Living Past.* Arco, 1979.

Hibard, Howard. *The Metropolitan Museum of Art.* Harper and Row, 1980.

Hirsh, Diana. and the Editors of Time-Life. *The World of Turner.* Time-Life Books, 1969.

Jacobson, Cliff. *The Basic Essentials of Map and Compass.* ICS Books, 1988.

Janson, H.W. *History of Art.* Harry N. Abrams Inc., 1974.

Janson, H.W. *History of Art.* Prentice Hall, 1991.

Leonard, Jonathon. *Norton and the Editors of Time-Life.* 1969.

Luard, Evan. *The United Nations How it Works and What it Does.* The Macmilan Press LTD., 1979.

Lyon, Sue. Editor. *The Italian Renaissance.* Marshall Cavendish, 1989.

Murray, Linda. *Michelangelo: His Life, Work and Times.* Thames and Hudson, 1984.

Schwartz, Gary. *Rembrandt.* Harry N. Abrams, 1992.

Smith, Bradley. *The USA. A History in Art.* Doubleday, 1982.

United Nations. *Your Nations The Official Guide Book.* U.N. Publications Board, 1987.

Webster's New Twentieth Century Dictionary of the Eight Language. The World Publishing Company, 1970.

Wedgwood, C. V. and the Editors of Time-Life. *The World of Rubens.* Time-Life Books, 1967.

Fiction

Holman, Felice. *Slake's Limbo.* Macmillan, 1986.

Peterson, P.J. *The Boll Weevil Express.* Dell, 1984.

Voigt, Cynthia. *Dicey's Song.* Macmillan, 1982.

Voigt, Cynthia. *Homecoming.* Macmillan, 1981.

Zindel, Paul, and Dragonwagon, Crescent. *To Take a Dare.* Bantam, 1984.

Answer Key

Page 10
1. Accept appropriate responses.
2. She felt she wasn't appreciated at home.
3. She enjoyed the planning of the adventure.
4. Wednesday, the day on which school had begun, was the start of Claudia's fiscal week.
5. Jamie was to go with her. They would go on Wednesday. They would take her violin case and his trumpet case packed with clean underwear. Jamie was to bring all of his money. They'd hide on the back seat of the school bus until the driver got off. Then they would ride the train on the ticket Claudia found in the wastebasket. They would stay in the Metropolitan Museum of Art.
6. Jamie got his money by saving his allowance and by cheating at cards.
7. In the blanket at the foot of his bed.
8. They hid in the back of the bus without making a sound.
9. He was carrying his money, $24.24, which was all in coins.
10. One letter was to their parents telling them not to call the FBI. The other one was two boxtops from corn flakes for a refund of twenty-five cents for milk.

Page 15
1. Accept appropriate responses.
2. A compass.
3. She said to stand on it…keep his head down. And keep the door to the booth very slightly open.
4. He controlled the money, and she promised that she would go along with any decisions that he made about spending.
5. They started feeling like a family of two, caring about each other, loving each other.
6. The murder of Amy Robsart, first wife of Lord Robert Dudley.
7. Claudia hid her violin case in a sarcophagus and her book bag behind a tapestry screen in the room of French furniture; the trumpet case was in a large urn. Jamie's book bag was behind a drape behind a statue from the Middle Ages.
8. She said they should learn and study art.
9. They toured the Egyptian wing by joining a visiting class of school children.
10. Accept appropriate responses.

Page 21
1. Accept appropriate responses.
2. They went to the library.
3. She told him to look through the books of photographs to find a picture of the angel statue.
4. Michelangelo.
5. He found the candy bar, and when Claudia was afraid to eat any of it, he bit off a piece and pretended to pass out.
6. The conversation was between two men discussing the angel statue and how they were going to move it to a different place.
7. They found money on the floor of the fountain and collected it. Accept appropriate responses regarding the honesty or dishonesty involved in taking coins from the fountain.
8. Three intersecting circles with an "M" inside one of them.
9. They discovered the meaning of the mark on the cover of a book in the bookshop.
10. The children sent a letter to the head of the museum. It told of Michelangelo's stone-mason's mark that they discovered on the bottom of the Angel.

Page 27
1. Accept appropriate responses.
2. They spent $4.50 for a post office box, but they knew they could get some more "income" from the bottom of the pool around the fountain.
3. They were Jamie's class from school.
4. He delivered it to the museum office.

Answer Key *(cont.)*

5. The boiler in the school furnace had broken, and there was no heat in the school, so classes were dismissed. He went into great detail about how it made a big explosion, fourteen kids were hurt, and parents were suing the school.

6. Claudia was intrigued because the guide was an Indian, wearing a sari. She was dressed differently than anyone Claudia knew.

7. Claudia wanted to move to a place where no one dressed like she dressed.

8. He did not carve the marble blocks which bore his mark, and someone else may have either carved the block or may have counterfeited his mark on the bottom of the statue.

9. She cried.

10. Accept responses which center on Claudia's desire to check out Mrs. Frankweiler.

Page 29

Page 32

1. Acceptappropriate responses.

2. A museum.

3. They were seeking information about the Italian Renaissance.

4. Accept responses including the following: filled with antique furniture; Oriental rugs; heavy chandeliers; office containing steel, Formica, vinyl, fluorescent lights, rows of filing cabinets; elegant bathroom with black marble walls, gold faucets, spigot shaped like a dragon's head, and huge black marble tub.

5. Jamie washed the palms of his hands, not the backs; Claudia took a bath.

6. Jamie accidentally told the secret of where they had been staying.

7. Claudia considered having the secret of it all the best part of running away.

8. She gave them one hour to find the secret file containing the answer.

9. She had a sketch of the angel drawn by Michelangelo in the file under Bologna.

10. She wanted to keep the secret.

Page 43

Matching

1. c	2. e
3. f	4. j
5. a	6. d
7. i	8. b
9. h	10. g

True or False

1. False	2. True
3. True	4. True
5. True	

The Short Answer

1. Greenwich
2. Secrets
3. They bathed in the pool around the fountain.
4. New York City
5. Michelangelo

Essay: Accept appropriate responses which explain how Claudia and Jamie became a team with extra credit for defining the word, "team."